D0066762

"Khadijah Queen's newest collection, *Anodyne*, is a study
of form & cavedwell, feminism as foresight, and archives the
articulation of black excellence & resilience. This is the complexity
fans of Queen's work have grown because of. How she shapes each
poem to the sound of a hand, photograph, fractured reflection, and
a throat. *Anodyne* as a noun is a painkilling medicine. These poems
are a painkilling medicine. They provoke, incite, and steer steady as
scripture. Each meter is breath, each beat encourages reassessment
by the reader unto themselves. Who we be beneath the dust & dust &
fallen arches of our name? Many (re)discoveries are assured
with the preciseness of Queen's poetic legend."

—MAHOGANY L. BROWNE, author of *Black Girl Magic*

"Khadijah Queen is a brilliant poet. I recommend this book
to anyone who ever had a child or a parent, who ever had a body or
loved, to anyone who was ever sick or tried to sleep a good night's
sleep, and failed, and tried again. . . . This is a powerful and dazzling
collection, filled with wisdom and experience. Anyone who reads
Anodyne will remember it for a long time."

—ILYA KAMINSKY, author of *Deaf Republic*

ANODYNE

ANODYNE

KHADIJAH QUEEN

TIN HOUSE / Portland, Oregon

Published by Tin House, Portland, Oregon

Distributed by W. W. Norton & Company

Library of Congress Cataloging-in-Publication Data

Names: Queen, Khadijah
Title: Anodyne / Khadijah Queen.
Description: Portland, Oregon : Tin House, [2020]
Identifiers: LCCN 2020004299 | ISBN 9781947793804 (paperback) |
 ISBN 9781947793903 (ebook)
Subjects: LCGFT: Poetry.
Classification: LCC PS3617.U443 A85 2020 | DDC 811/.6—dc23
LC record available at https://lccn.loc.gov/2020004299

First US Edition 2020
Printed in the USA
Interior design by Jakob Vala

www.tinhouse.com

COVER:
Romare Bearden, *Untitled (Woman with Flower)*, 1969. Collage on Masonite, 23 5/8 × 17 1/2 in. (60 x 44.5 cm). The Studio Museum in Harlem; gift of anonymous donor; 1976.52 © Romare Bearden Foundation / VAGA at Artists Rights Society (ARS), NY

for Kim Smith—
for your brilliance & enduring belief

CONTENTS

Painkillers only put me in the twilight

—Kendrick Lamar

We know ourselves as part and as crowd,
in an unknown that does not terrify.

—Édouard Glissant

Wasn't it you who told me civilization is
impossible in the absence of a spirit of play.

—Anne Carson

IN THE EVENT OF AN APOCALYPSE, BE READY TO DIE

But do also remember galleries, gardens,
herbaria. Repositories of beauty now
ruin to find exquisite—

untidy, untended loveliness of the forsaken,
of dirt-studded & mold-streaked
treasures that no longer belong to anyone

alive, overrunning
& overflowingly unkempt monuments to
the disappeared. Chronicle the heroes & mothers,
artisans who went to the end of the line,

protectors & cowards. Remember
when pain was not to be seen or looked at,
but institutionalized. Invisible, unspoken,

transformed but not really transformed. Covered up
with made-up valor or resilience. Some
people are not worth saving, no one wants

to say, but they say it in judgment. They say it
in looking away. They say it in staying safe in a lane
created by someone afraid of losing ground,

thinking—*I doubt we're much to look at,*
as we swallow what has to hurt until we can sing
sharp as blades. Aiming for the sensational

as we settle for the ordinary, avoiding
evidence of suffering at all costs, & reach
clone-like into the ground as aspen roots, or slide

feet first down a soft slope, wet, cold—but the faith
to fall toward the unseen, the bleak of most
memory—call it elusive. Call it the fantasy to end

all fantasies, a waiting fatality, blight of both
education & habit. Warned inert,
we could watch ourselves, foolish, lose it all.

OF ALL THE THINGS I LOVE

My son wants to leave, depression making

talk of permanent exit a habit. I make him

laugh, a temporary stay, spend every penny

I have to keep him in the comfort and joy

of computer games and good eating—his idea,

anyway, fried and meaty and overdosing

on pancakes and Golden Oreos and steamed

chocolate with whole milk. I don't drink much,

but I want to. Since last summer the Woodford

only halved. *Why can't I be myself in this world*,

over and over he asks me, knowing I'm powerless

everywhere except home regardless of what I say.

I would move the fucking universe for you, I say,

as many times as I have to, and we both know how

fragile my body is compared to my mind. My energy

never stopped fueling two. He likes to humor me.

He knows better and has the scars to prove it,

but he believes I will try, having never seen me give up

without a fight that ended in the wreck of someone else,

even if it cost me, too. Sunlight debilitates him and night

keeps him angry awake. How do I tell him that I'm tired?

EROSION

10 million years casts any movement as given. Grand Mesa—prone

to rockslide but craters at Dotsero stay young. Once,

lava flow took a mile of highway, stretched out its red heat & black

smoke rising grey to white, no lake, crawling baby of magma

& water. When snow-topped, both still boom with basalt.

That molten underground we swim the surface of.

In Palisade the low range casts no shadow over the vines, peaks

rising inward as separate entities, stark high earth and low-height

green. Road dust cradles the ground. I go there with a friend

                                    A drink in the evening

becomes two, laughter then a free confession overlooking lavender

fields—man-made, another desert verdanted, in which one person

admits they are precious enough to hide—the night brings out hunters—intoning survival in that shadow, blink of life in swallow

& vapor, body ever in revolt, a red centimeter of a mouth

asking what else. How we fail is how we continue.

DOUBLE WINDLASS

after Pizarnik & McMorris

under volcanic moonshadow	double twilight took	the honeycomb infatuates
city moss *in lateral sail*	chapels bees grotto— *whitelit*	
invocations—	on dawn's broad summit	a glad populace afar *a whole-mouthed sea*

LIVE UNADORNED

Turn the wake
sublime—

Identify a new habit
in progress   a good succulent
in a sea of smooth pebbles

A sky can be grey
even in a warm
off-season

In defiance of time
the smallest people   dance in it
naturally

They want to
have the last sound

MONOLOGUE FOR PERSONAE

Disguised as an I *(no direction)*   we say:
Hello, disarray. Soft hip abridged, subaltern superstructure—

We came to exist   *in apparent psychological systems*
We arrived starlit, not dust-borne, ending in decayed light

Under certain circumstances, we sit in drawings
like some old sir, as cold as refusal, wingless.

We came with merchant discipline. Light with stealth, in our anti-prime.
Implicit: private rages to thwart

most paramount wants, sultanistic
without asking, outside time, inside unknown

epochs. We created ourselves out of
parking lots, an organized chorus repeating *I want to go home*

In varying intonations, with variant urgencies,
we came to *(no direction)*   *the opposite of illusion*

We came to silken the asterism
We came drunk off sea liquor to unravel threads of flesh

We came to be shaped, enough repetition
We came to be in flux, unnamed, then pronounced by care

We came to have our newness used up by the wrong power,
We came to be tucked back into embrace

We came to shutter the past in our ignorance
We came to shutter the past in our enlightenment

(Black box / Red chair / Red flowers on a table,
dead or alive. Some spiraling of strange light)

COPPER MEN

As an afterthought

bring you bent wires to

cuff your small wrists.

Think delicate bones

under soft flesh when

it dawns in some far

latitude where you are not

forgettable yet. Accept

every offered scrap—

talk, metal, touch. Exchange

twisted infinitudes learned hard

ways, flake & tarnish.

For the next artisan, you

forge a mulish silver

preference—by no known

means compliant

SOMETHING ABOUT THE WAY I AM MADE IS NOT MADE

to make sense—I stretch my insides

across pages until my pain is upside down. Peonies &

tulips bloom red & pink from my back,

bent like washerwomen's knees—

full-on shadow. But I could have neon

feathers if I wanted—faux

apparatus of flight. I could have cultivated in error

the bad luck of odd numbers.

      Spectators claim

ancestral innocence, as ever—a suit

two sizes too small for escape & inside the coveted

dance, I first look down at extraneous steps

in shame. For all my notes

& vices, I still long to stop the false

fight for my humanity, en masse, allowed to share

a history of anything but suffering

DEMENTIA IS ONE WAY TO SAY FATAL BRAIN FAILURE

Whose mind loses when

the loved decline.

Human by whose degrees. Capability

and refusal twined up in

loose fog, time-shocked. A body is what

without its engine. How do I let go of my mother

before she is gone? Predator grief doesn't watch,

yellow-eyed, from hidden grasses

like a real apex. We slow-feed that wraith. Viscera.

I HAVE A METHOD OF LETTING GO

Asthmatic child in a house full of smokers, I crawled once
under toxic clouds to find my mother

I was so brave I almost died, or desperate

I wanted her more than breath
I was so small & she could sing
anything alive, almost

She didn't really know, doesn't know now—

She is familiar with duty & made me so
I can't live on that loss

In 1977 a bullet turned my brother into dust
His 18 years here, an invisible talisman we hold in our callous living

Sometimes I think my mother smoked to pretend to breathe him in

A TINY NOW TO FEED ON

So clear the heart after
the unreal takes up—

I've not learned
what to sew besides
more, other scars—

how to live *exuberant with settle*
too much room
underneath skin   *feels like crossing*

to stay golden   Seconds wasted
count as wanting, preening

o reactionary
hushes, mean illusory
I held close or trashed
in fear *The Great American terrain*

I can't carry without my spine
        —*gold rings, bare wrists*

weakening at pressure
points I don't tend often

enough. I take all
    A break is just the space

between a cutting,
my skin holds, try not to

think about withering, *a potion for*
whatever you don't want—belonging
in failed ways,

failure meaning a field

wrecked by birds
or a field meaning nothing.
If in the air, believe
In my body pitch

selfishness as religion   Devotion at least,
knifelike, everything else abraded,

even the sky, that sear

HORIZON ERASURE

Blue-grey braceleted   Hollow

               torrent threat

comes on   cloud shift. What about letting go

              Ivy clung to passageway ceilings, some grass on

      shoes   Untied

                         Blood moon

tried to take my son

             Stop refusing to understand

UT PICTURA POESIS

How do I fancy a good atonement Homebound body
so slow to bounce back from overuse, meaning, darling,

A cuff of immensity threads me—   centrifugal
I could fragment thus *a rifle shard in a blood flick, dew*
perched upon arrival
       Where travel is a future &
not such arts
as ordinary inheritance *azure mass—explicit menace*
   in a wing lull I try not to take
My mother, grandmother for granted
& not their elegant fierceness in flight— How do

I resurrect the excised archive of my relatives
       How to use the word
love, mean it *my animal glow—sacred rot*
This luxury of time to even ask: Who were they

X

In Blombos Cave an etching—

a cave of swimmers. a lake of sand dunes. in every rock a green
across the first continent.
100 years / 100,000—collapsed

gesture learned, the mark
of wanting to make marks in the surrounding
objects to say: *what?*

X

what once marked the body?—too much
pressed into bones—
ancient value feels hopeful, the Blackest millennia
so vindicated. an ochre block & a herd of cattle sweep across
     hyperbolic

pastoral, a history
in skin   in blood   in everything alive a disturbance

THE RULE OF OPULENCE

Bamboo shoots on my grandmother's side path
grow denser every year they're harvested for nuisance.
Breezes peel blush and white petals from her magnolia,
lacing unruly roots in the spring grass. For nine decades
she has seen every season stretch out of shape, this past
Connecticut winter slow to relinquish cold. As a girl
she herded slow turkeys on her aunt Nettie's farm, fifty acres
in a Maryland county that didn't plumb until midcentury,
plucking chickens and pheasants from pre-dawn
into the late night, scratching dough
for neighbors, relatives stopping by for biscuits, and the view
from my window changes. It's Mother's Day
and I'd always disbelieved permanence—newness a habit,
change an addiction—but the difficulty of staying put
lies not in the discipline of upkeep, as when my uncle chainsaws
hurricane-felled birches blocking the down-sloped driveway,
not in the inconvenience of well water
slowing showers and night flushes, not in yellowjackets
colonizing the basement, nuzzling into a hole
so small only a faint buzz announces their invasion
when violin solos on vinyl end, but in the opulence of acres
surrounding a tough house, twice repaired from fires, a kitchen
drawer that hasn't opened properly in thirty years marked *Danger*,
nothing more permanent than the cracked flagstone
path to the door, that uneven earth, shifting.

ANTEDILUVIAN

Where were you when the truth disappeared or

when the truth battered us & we pretended fear

fell from the ripped pillow of our sky instead of

rising up from the one clear place of us   Where

were you when strongmen told us to die &

blasted us into nothing   Were you downtown

to witness the smooth mirage   stagnate in sky-

scraper shade & neon glower   Did you hop a bus

& clutch a cold center rail, the sweat of your palm

making you slip as if at sea   Were you at sea

in memory, gathered into lyric, your body

pretending any era was a safe one   Six persimmons

ripen unconsumed, mayfly wings flash

their iridescence in the dark   Nothing works

By swallowing alarm   you scrapped what you knew

near plaza fountains, ultra-anonymous

Now   an arrowhead sharpens

the blood under our flesh   Low to the ground,

a sea of tamarisks   You claim millennia

led to the false obelisks   led to what severs

the head of connection in the time of least   But we

only ask   that you not kill us

SESTINA FOR PERSONAE

We choose to call our scatter

Expansion—openness, inexact song,

        Imaginative loop

We came to what wants to surface—

The rest revealed in undercurrents, our bodies

Insistent

Insistent

No one in charge but energy   We arrived to scatter

With half the clamor of bodies,

     Screaming or singing

For the throat's own sake, its corrugated surface—

We arrived luxuriating in the loop

(light moves downstage right in a frantic loop

Improvisational movement or complete stillness, insistent)

We came to *(improvisational movement or complete stillness)* surface

We came to be anywhere—to scatter

Paint but not trash, to turn holographic, singing

It's not true that we miss what we can't give our bodies

We came to say there's another, plusher approach—bodies

(Bromeliads appearing in the staged darkness, in silver, variegated,

    yellow loops)

(Improvisational movement or low volume singing)

Mean what they are—insistent

When we say we want, the love in it—absent the scatter

We came to deny the surface

We came to be impossible and surfaced

Inside Emily Dickinson's perfect attitude, our bodies

Longing—for what? A defect as power, scattering

Ruthless integrity in a joyful time loop

We came to consider anything alive respectable, insistent

Anyone in need of radical devotion can or not sing

We came to choose *(indiscernible mumbling or opera singing*

& unrestrained laughter) chocolate cosmos, floriphages, all summer surfaces

Maintained in drought, anything we can count on—*(folds into self)* insistent

We came through the Taghkanic in autumn, our bodies

Arrived in red deer abiding a clear path, a loop

Arriving nowhere, but scatter—

Who are we? Orion songs, missed evergreens, bodies

Looped into every surface, looped

Insistent into struggle—like heirloom seeds, rising in scatter

SKY ERASURE

sans bright star equivalent, hoist

autumn slate

    & dive up, cloud borne

hooked for purchase, flail

lark limbed at song   ,

    at light bridge, try rocket—

every angular distance boxed under

constellations three fists apart

SYNESTHESIA

I. *Theory*

First, I was twenty-five with no sleep   (   )

&   my body said   feel this   And I didn't

want to   (   ) then   It turned into a constant &   (   )

burned to be felt   I couldn't harden

away from it   couldn't ease   (   )

or sleep   or not-feel   my way away   because (   )

   it was myself &

what my child could see   (   )   & what   I was
   watching   (   )

Semiotics—

a feeling as dagger   (   )   as gestural shard

sheathed expensively   (   )   dividing itself from its origins

from evidence of uncertain shifts   (   )

Dreams for three nights: I sang *hush* to a wounded man

                    (   )

                    (   )

gunshots, my brother   (   )   and he lived. I said a

   prayer &

a ghost running crowded   (   )   woke up calm.

Streets and shady hallways.   I severed

the angriest part of me   (   )

                       only to have double the raging

(   )

              weapons grow in its place

II. *Signification + Gesture Drawing*

A mechanism crumbling its history, I used to

(   ) build up my own hard feelings   (   )   with

   those of

others   Can you believe

I   (signifier)   would take them   like they were mine

   or take them

like I could take them   away   (   )

   like I could

learn   the texture of a heart   as if touching it   (   )

in the dark like in   *Grey's Anatomy*

      when the power went out   (   )

Dr. Yang has to put her hand inside   a man to feel

where the hole is, feel   how to save his life

& now I   (   )   sketch a tender gesture:

smell of antiseptic as   the squeezing of a lover's hand versus

grinding against   a stranger's crotch   *ondulato*

ODE TO 180 PAIRS OF WHITE GLOVES

smacking that ass

making a phat beat

(the thinking man's Beyoncé

endlessly sketching

Isaach de Bankolé)

O hair as urgent bulletin

cosmic drifts of hair

emitting *important information*

O untapped talents and salted bravado

a syntactic turn-on

a paragraphic chasm

stirring up hallucinogenic

invader magic

resembling a hoarded apocalypse

of fetishized resistance

against a corridor of wounds

O honeypot hand in a real

busy honeycomb

watching the bees

suck on brown girls' legs—sharp

like hustlers   or suicidal stargazers

O pink lips first pulling on a Kool

I DREAMT YOU AT THE TATE

Leaned forward on a long bench, long legs

taking up the whole sleek area

Drawing your own sneakers & eating a tuna melt

cut in half

After you offered me that 50%

I took out my own giant sketchpad & we switched—

Size 14 men's & size 7.5 women's, archival

Who cares about matching

The dream occurred on a plane

traveling north from Phoenix to Denver & now

carouseling slow is my neutral hardside

& Sade, through Bluetooth, intends to leave like a lion

RETREAT

If I had the bones for this, I could cheat

the finish. Melodramatically, die

trembling as I peel tangerines

in a state, catering to doubt.

A lifetime thinking *I know who I*

am here—I avoided erasure, I fought—

Can I collect my fragments,

fragile now in the gentleness

your questions taught?

No such marginalia. In every burst

of agreement, no turbulence to try

& estrange us, no opposition to

map onto the joke. Observe

the rough architecture a whole person

bases key decisions on,

its faulty edges hazed against

clarity, uncut nails

catching on unfortunate silk—

RECLUSIONARY

Stranger, the stone forest

alive with limestone

says come on over to my place

à la Pendergrass & watch the LCD TV

but only 'til I die & not after

None of that Poe shit

Let's watch animal gods meanwhile

probe the floodplains—

red in beak & claw

How else can I live alone

having read ol' Herm through 1857

Knowing what's corroded its way

into the heart itself—the entrance

full of swifts, Archimedes counting

principles of loss & we can get joy

clocking subterranean

pursuits of cave-evolved fish on *Nat Geo*

IN THE QUIET

I ended things & need to migrate soon

I've had a rocky epoch

Not boring & non-hairsplitting so

resort to heating leftovers in the oven

Or in a blue skillet on a hot eye

Watch a wasp behind blinds escape

Laconic ease in the new absence,

so beigy safe & later, fiddleheaded

Souped-up in a fast sleep

I furl at the least pain

For fun & distraction—*American Horror Story*

Violence I can turn off

DECLINATION

The truth is I *am* lionhearted. Dreaming
no match for the waking flame. We fell asleep smelling smoke,
placed damp towels on all the sills. Now the ground is frozen
and in the dream, distance evaporates. I say every word
held back, bold in touch too, lengthening in spirit. The mountains
shadow the rust of the cold day breaking and we hum with energy. Winter
keeps us lucky, rested, like suns.

Are you an eagle yet?
Serpents, they say, can't keep
lies from breaking their tongues. In the dream I resist
your silence protects me
from my own. One touch to eradicate all sense except, electric,
what you know you control.

On a day like this, mottled grey-blue with threats of yellow,
I watercolor until hunger overtakes. I might write but words don't feel
brave enough.
Do you draw upon waking? Do you first spike a coffee or
rinse dreams from your skin with wet heat? I dare not ask. I make. I make
messes I delight in. I draw, too,
darken my small hands with charcoal, blow its dust
off the paper, use up chamois after chamois
deepening shadows, black as lust. Or ink. Sleek
lines improvised across the cotton rag. Why can't this work
make me not want you drawn

over me, a dream in rowdy fragments, impossible. Midwinter
the day thrilled frozen, denatured minute by minute
into a graveyard for night and dreams.
I could want you or hate that want. I heat
last night's plate just as light snakes in. I add lemon to the cool
water in a faceted glass. Set it down heavy, ringing the wood.

My sister would tell me
I need to stay focused. I do.

I am writing this in the creeping dawnstrokes, having made my list
and folded the white paper into crude fourths. I have to manage.

Foolish, I know, to try so many times
after spectacular failure. But I refuse to fight the urge to
rise from my low camouflage, letting hunger quicken the hunter in me,
shattering pretense. I make a show, don't I, blushed
and modest even as I etch your departing silhouette in gold.

IF GOLD, YOUR FIGURE AS MIRROR ON THE GROUND IS

after Pizarnik, after Pessoa

I.

Comic screen to change what came to notice Even though sky
at first was the same blank slate So literal. The value of it

You make your own lion's teeth sink in, slowly

II.

So green the insects claim you don't belong here
then bite & bite

Virtue the undulant yards as penance

III.

The capuchin stays silent in the void

You feel the sun of unknown experiments

IV.

Hordes of animals without teeth crash the window in a
dream & it means you are not hungry enough

V.

Once a choice comes to full & the act carries the joy
of struggle The winter mother severs only a chance at
restarting. Could you sorrow the one unchosen thing
infinitely so it feels occasional, the act is itself

VI.

Where the jewelry case in your closet holds
Not expensive things but purchased—
Acquired in a place that no longer exists

If I write a texture I could make it stucco like childhood
Aloe or cactus spines / to cut is to heal the rough of a cut
All dark blue against good skin like leather

VII.

Aloud your voice heightens its wrongness
You speak anyway because you are learning / I think this might be the
end of insecurity

VIII.

Imagine the root of oppositional archetypes Next to me
chrysanthemums the rust of blood when it dries but in front of me So
much blue & a broken white

I can't see myself on purpose

IX.

What rocks itself out of time on a wing beat Is not a
    name or a silence

As in sanity's meager gestures. Downriver, the unruly
    sound turned
C-shaped / Real secrets as fragrant & familiar as
    what's under the smoke

                       I stand next to the rocks
Where you choose to return without choosing / Some black,
    some silver
The lines of ash & passage A neon swig of enlightenment

X.

Don't be exceptional in this false.
All fluent in nothing, hiding where your debt grows

Be aggressive or do not mind, you say

I feel like a chicken after boiling
Or like you do now—smooth from the pain

        (I love how you love promises because they are lies)
        (I love the honesty of cheap rings)

    Like a ripened plum or two, pitted—Now a flat middle ground, now
        another
    interior to hold the ruin

XI.

Your hair grows in eighths on alternate days but you pretend not to count What rains in it

What grandiose adornment hasn't happened but will happen Also a lie—in color

XII.

The grunting you hear on the other side of the wall might be music Or
the disaster of a concrete floor

The western cities, the eastern cities / I chose that inscrutable skin
The high ground of resurrection Discursive—
falling soft / I witness the guilt planted for others

I practice by moving my legs I am a bracket
You are the conquering seawall

Nothing earth about you except what clean is visible Also your hands

ECLOGUE FOR PERSONAE

All the way human, we came to hurt.
We came via unpredictable route
via safer lacuna, via habit of wondering
what desire settles belief in commitment,
in silence & self-observation

We came to shell the day-cold,
bone-filled, language-less

We arrived in winter,
a snow-topped mountain range spilled
adrenaline through the bay window
samaras of white ash

We arrived with varied intensity
As in to make a disturbance

We came when our eyes burned
& consent to what we don't know
how to heal yet
We allow for devastation

Discomfort is for the machine's sake
meant to break you or part of you—
We are not asking

It feels strange to smile in a fascist era—grief
dammed up, ancient energy held back
like certain floods

We have flooded ourselves, we have flooded

Nine hazel trees & a mother's
body as a door of no return
A mother's body as a place we've been
mapped inside of, a galaxy

pointing toward grit,
& who can feel the possible
in their bodies & not break
toward it—

(Any closing action)

THE WORLD SAYS NOT TO EXPECT THE WORLD

But do it anyway—   be made, all

out of love—   taken, bestowed, lived

through, by means of, without

the beauty we don't want

to waste   & the world says it

wants, but trashes, sees as glut, usable

in a finite manner   We like talk

of human   forevers as holes in us

unfilled, we're raggedy apartments

Which thin glamour to blame for such

schism, runaways   & orchids

tattooed on wrists or thighs, as dull men scoff—

We still say   keep fighting

& love me again—   don't the pines die, too

& exactly   with our names

I WATCH EXACT IN DISCONNECT

after Anaximander & McMorris

futile a cartographer's dream to	
graph	material persistence
	of faults

ODE TO THE ACCURACY OF INTUITION

O collagist   O montage maker of scenes

ancient & modern & profane, O superimposer of meaninglessness

    upon the voiceless

       tormented in the gloss

of daily rags, O the figures   magnificently

    gowned in the explosion

          precious untouched, O but not the women whose

children fly

    limbless into sky or earth

       as men watch or die or kill, O

painter of rainbows in soldiers' hands, O gluer of Caucasian smiles

             against atomic skies, O

    Febrezer of Iraq,

       O arranger of models lounging legs open

      in the war zone, bare-assed models in the kitchen

          on fire, cloned acrobats in the verdant 1970s

    fields, fake-lashed

fine line of the tightest rope,

    O if you left them a net, O a sea of ocelots beneath it

———

PRECIPITATION ERASURE

Rain—   blackening

what's already slick, dark in ice walk

season—   slip

free into whose choice

A script you   glove up for, in spiral.

That small   home

folding screams into lace. Permeable,

evaporating—

ANODYNE

I wish I'd learned to take better care

As if this world tried to love me
A body I used up
on hard ground, flowsy &
sop-studded, misplacing words

I keep to settle for pain

Pitch breaks in—
body leaning into quiet
I couldn't ask for, what I needed

& thought I couldn't afford. A shun,
undone, a hush a shudder through

thinned fascicles of flesh &
flimsy bone, walkward
in a lost idiom. Are we on a heartway?
We could pretend. Calculate

how immaculate hardship
covets itself

Acts like it aches for more

IMMINENCE

Bergen County, New Jersey

A pair, young, embrace—heels lift,
arms encircle, not expecting
lifetimes to come next, bodies grown taller

in a blink, imagine they've yet to be
pulled by the wrist into supermarkets,
by the hair into adolescence,

by the sorrow-struck heart into graffiti or frantic
streets, dim & touch-starved, can we? If
even our buried objects strike us

as reversal of sky, & we look down
only in the wrong seasons
at what sustains our weight

& containment means existing inside, & when
we contain we are contained in time, in place,
in memory, those immensities

we forbid ourselves, so vast
our resistance as infinite tininess, defiance
an Atlantic problem, hallucination, worse,

cello-soundtracked—a course of recovery
amid strewn bricks, dead acres &
plastic-laden foliage trudging

along the Passaic, past wrought-
iron fences green with corrosion, foresight absent
denial—choices to make for the labyrinth

NJ TRANSIT PASSENGER ODE

On the way home from the MoMA I decide

I want those blue patent leather peep-toe

stilettos & hardback Japanese novel with silver

bookmark scissored dead center

I want vegetarian gumbo

I want snapper & trout blackened on the spit

I want feet that don't swell &

veins that don't threaten varicosity

I want that lean man to kiss me

on the back of the neck & smile

when he whispers, so I can feel what he means

between breaths—the truth of all performance

I want that heiress ease

minus the trickle-down

I want to clear the Lincoln Tunnel

Shit I want 24-hour service

to be unnecessary

I want to sleep at night

& when I do I want dreams

like the one last April

My family all lived

in the same place

long enough to grow daffodils & safe babies

I want to know

who's walking toward them on the street

I want a real salve, a cool

wet cloth & jasmine tea

I want to bow down with

my arms breaking earth

until it grows more delicious

than shaved dimes between

my grandmother's teeth

I want the city's lights to stop

telling me that bedtime story—the song

I can't get enough of—the swagger

keeping me hooked

ANCIENT MOTHER I KEEP TEACHING US NEW WAYS TO FIND JOY

I draw no propriety *My island is recursive*   So I have a son
whose brilliance   :   :
isn't understood yet   I know how to make a frail body
look perfect   but not a sad mind or a world
that can't catch up   Since I cannot run

I stretch   my thoughts fight   my voice
low *like water in air*   *extinction*

: *what continuum* :   I return
fallen   My illnesses in secular lifetimes—no matter
Sound makes space in the throat   *in a glint euphonic*

small lights free affection   I face
those prepared for open force   those who favor weapons
My caution limited
to what might exhaust this brittle form, easily spent
muscles, bones ready to snap *How to weasel a monsoon*

I have instead
50 ways to plummet   if I slip twice
will it rain again before   : the Trance :   How is joy

a ruptured curse   if I get more tattoos as a crone
will my withering get more or less   respect *from whom*
I didn't perceive where imaginary lives cacophonized

into the real   How my skin handles certain atrophy is akin to
what I devote to trust   How does one outstretch the practical
in hiding from husbandry   A violin can whistle

if you want it to *The sun a warm tint on a bad photograph* Who am I
without this danger   & with this naiveté, protected still

I'm sitting too long
Of what   would I be afraid

AFTERLIGHT ERASURE

The pain   is   willing   &

                                                I suffer—

                A good mother does   what it takes.

                                        privilege made peace with

                                trust.
        Sometimes   force

                                                        means react right—

                                        Right of escape   until
        that body has fled. Until that scene

                                        eludes
        jubilance—

                                                what's left

COMMON MIRACLES

Across the definition of blue   A dozen

Rave in disappearing patterns—
            Quarrel of sparrows

Branches beam full green
Bebel sings   A falling star is here   & with us
cavaquinho, fado, mandolin

Invisibly   A cracked bone stitches itself a whitened scar
over and over—caixa wires

Breath culled under   cuica, timbal

A wasp on the stone poolside   for a monument

I WATCH THE ENDLESS BREAKAGE OF WINGS

after Mothlight *&* McMorris

the light beauty death sped up	blue-black the sepia
the white behind translucence	the rage the whirl of it
like falling like a false flight	

ROUTE

Unlit, we left
at break, rode south
Turned hard

left up canyon, up
rockslide-paved wind-sown
center of buttes

Lungs opened
to river down into
cut cliffs

White-topped
energy shift
over plain hills   Played over
steep rock vein

Cut body
coming to memory as arid
An astonishing

Sea of sagebrush, sand,
low forest of scrub pine

Tough piñon
Failing as cow shade
A rural rust

Cloud shadows' chatoyancy
veneers mid-range peaks
Radiant as green rise
Laneside

Acres, acres of which
We cannot
divine from dust

Terrain blue from
sky influence
A true mesa
Crow on the median

Perfect light-leveling rock
jut & lone antelope
facing fallen gates

Trailers left beside
a homeless staircase
Music changes

at the boundary imagined
between horses &
housing debris
Who can live

Next to what's falling apart

DOUBLE LIFE

Last night I split a bottle
plus a glass of white, a clear
Cali sauv that first woke me then
put me to sleep. In between

bites of poblano soup & spicy
slaw on bootleg street tacos we ran
off each random white man who thought
he could eat in our silence

with our crass laughter & endless
sentences about oppression in work
life & bloodstreams, ours & others'
& who did they think could escape now,

collision of fear & brazenness
clapping together in historical play
across the moving planet. Erika says

a woman named Chocoletta
saved her from boss-led persecution
& I say or think something like

Her mother had vision
& the power in a Black woman's name
saves us all. Hungover & overworked

this morning I get my tax bill. Doubled
my income last year, so owe double too.
I wish I could pull a Thoreau but
I'm only 41.8% white. If only I could just be

chased off a bar stool at The Hornet
on Broadway after eating a plate of fake nachos
& drinking a warm pilsner. Instead I fear
the end of a chase ending in blood,
mine or someone I love & I love us all

& so many of my white friends know
how to help ease my way out of wreck. I show up
at the university in bold new professor

leather & tweed, elbow-patched & afraid I'll learn to
pontificate too much by default, or tell
too much truth, or be much too
Black to be trusted. I notice

one of my white male students leaves the room
every time we talk about race. My therapist tells me
I should put things like that in the container

I made up for what I can't control & I do. This job
isn't writing at all & I'm burning
too fast, afraid to combust &
afraid I won't. For dessert we split

peach cobbler topped with vanilla ice cream.
I don't eat dairy so she spooned it up & I basked

in the warm sugar & fruit & surprise of
caramel crisscrossed on the just-right crust,
remembering my grandmother & the smell of
nutmeg & cinnamon in her kitchen, fresh peaches

simmering in syrup in an old pot on the gas stove,
her fingers pinching quick dough, remembering
her permanent frown as a pair of mirrored crescents
between her eyes, the map of lines on her forehead,

& as we speak I am inheriting the furrows
earned rightfully by crones. If you do it quickly,
Grandma said, you can heal burns without leaving a scar.
Smooth your injured skin then peel

& cut a potato in two
& hold each rinsed half to the heated flay
until the potato turns black. Repeat
until it looks like nothing ever happened.

Uncle Sugarpie raised her
& her sisters in Michigan because white men
lynched her father in Alabama & threatened
her uncle with death if he didn't leave, too.

They took my great-grandfather's store & land & home &
Uncle Sugarpie was a nice man but rocked
on his front porch chair with a shotgun if he saw

any white men walking the neighborhood trying to sell
any damn thing. What else can we do
for protection? I think about that in the ecstasy
of a sweet peach & irony of death & theft of indigenous
land & the violence of language in every space

I enter & I think I am losing everything but my mind.
I certainly am paying for the trouble

& we split all that liquor so now
our whispers mean to get loud. Yes, now
you have to listen, or move the hell out of the way.

EPILOGUE FOR PERSONAE

We came to the past, at night, in some future access point,
Moonless. We hold no blame
For attachment past attachment's end,

We show up to show how we arrive—
A path to lose our sense of others

We came to paint neon text
On a black wall with a ten-foot paintbrush, rhapsodic
We came to find out when molecules touch & almost react

We came to approach green with shaped blue or flood
The field pink, its shapes folding, the page weight

Undoing weightlessness, opposites
Allowed to oppose in peace,
Reflective counterpoint

Imagining

I SLEPT WHEN I COULDN'T MOVE

Black girl, black girl

Don't lie to me

Tell me where

Did you sleep last night

    —Leadbelly, "Black Girl (In the Pines)"

I slept in my own bed in need of replacement

I slept sitting up against a steel bunk in Illinois winter next to military
    strangers

I slept beneath a run of pipes on a destroyer & I slept with a failed guitarist

I slept on his brocade couch in the Valley & left before I could
    remember his face

I slept in the deepest part of Watts

in my lover's grandmother's house

with a view of an abandoned lot overgrown with weeds & drug trash

He kept his mouth persistent & unfamiliar

In a dark turn I slept in a bathtub dispossessed

I slept with love & treated myself to unkindness

I slept after repeating myself alone & I slept in a friend's guest room
    with a broken window

& listened to nameless strays killing what they eat it's hard work

When I was small I slept with three sisters the same size in a house
    with the gas cut off

I slept with a man who hated himself & we slept in a beautiful bed in a
    loft with a downtown view

& he brought me red wine & cold water

I slept happily in hotels when I could escape

I slept in a mountain cottage & wrapped myself in a crocheted blanket &
    sorrow & wrote poems about
my animus
I slept on the floor in my father's house I never slept in the brick
one-story my grandfather built & sometimes I feel like concrete
I slept in the palm of my own Black hand
I slept when I couldn't move
I slept in a place that hadn't been built yet & dreamt the sheer violence of
    the future
I slept inside a song with a Blacker voice than mine which meant I slept good
I slept in the orange light of day silence
I never slept on the street
I slept in the knotted hair of my sister's children in Detroit & washed &
    combed it in the morning
I slept when I couldn't move
I slept in a California desert, free of bodies & trees
I slept in senescent lake muck
I slept through earthquakes & El Niño & never stopped traveling

I slept in my car on the side of Fountain Street at dawn & my car shook
    from the traffic but I worked all night & couldn't wake up
I slept in a rented studio apartment in Brooklyn with roaches & the
    aroma of methamphetamines
climbing through vents & under the door & dreamt about work
I slept to the repetition of Cesária Évora
I slept on a feather bed & let myself dream a cracked blue

I slept in a red dress & sparrows woke me in the morning

I slept in a black dress & saw a hawk in my grandmother's magnolia

I slept in my beauty & in sleep I knew that beauty as inheritance

couldn't be stolen or strung up or caged or appropriated effectively &
 it's mine

& what I have to own I have to love it

I slept where I was born & a rude wind pushed me into exile

I slept in the infinite arrangements of Prince's instruments

I slept out of dreams when cranes cut the sky in an era of smog

I slept in San Joaquin farm country & there were too many kinds of
 molesters

I slept when I couldn't move

I slept in on a Sunday next to the radio

I slept crying every night for a year when I failed at my best thing but
 I kept him alive

I slept in a world I forgot to love sometimes

I slept as if I still believed in rescue

I slept expensively & poorly & middle class

I slept when I couldn't afford to

I slept in stolen freesia

I slept for a moment in snow & reclamation

I slept in *Hejira* & wasn't cruel when I slept

I slept in kinship with my faults

In a dream I was hopeful & slept when I needed a radical silence

I slept next to a man's portrait with someone else & more than once I
 didn't close my eyes

I slept in a lie & the comfort felt so real it was real

I slept as if I were years

I slept so many years I couldn't find

In sleep my eyes dreamt the nearness of waiting & couldn't touch it

I slept in the clues I couldn't wake from

I slept in hidden cameras & microphones

I slept in secret & in public

I slept so sure in a used place & so anonymous like womanhood & so
    hypervisible I slept in a kind of fire & became it

I slept in a place of brilliant bones & the future of Blackness

I slept in a system outside of every law but one

I slept when I couldn't move

I slept in a simple way

I slept in a place just for us

I slept where I could see it

NOTES & ACKNOWLEDGMENTS

The Lamar quote is from the song *Alright*; the Glissant quote is from *Poetics of Relation*, translated by Betsy Wing; the Carson quote is from *The Beauty of the Husband*.

"In the event of an apocalypse, be ready to die" appears in *Boston Review*'s chapbook, *Poems for Political Disaster* (2017).

"Double windlass," "Ut pictura poesis," and "Ancient mother I keep teaching us new ways to find joy" appear in *Inverted Syntax* (October 2018, January 2019).

McMorris is a reference to Mark McMorris, particularly his grid poems in *The Book of Landings*. *Mothlight* is a 1963 short film by Stan Brakhage.

The Poetry Review (UK) published "Live unadorned," "Something about the way I am made is not made," and an earlier version of "Anodyne" in Autumn 2017.

"Monologue for personae" and the other *personae*-titled poems are after Fernando Pessoa, Lucille Clifton's "the message from The Ones," Robert Hayden's *American Journal*, and Mahmoud Darwish's *In the Presence of Absence*.

"Dementia is one way to say fatal brain failure" was written after reading the official language around Alzheimer's disease and dementia—the reductiveness and violence of the medical terminology adds a dehumanizing dimension to the already difficult process of understanding the diagnosis and its real-life ramifications. We all lose when we are failed by our healthcare system and the language it uses to describe us and our bodies.

The erasure poems and poems with italicized text are culled from various guidebooks, dictionaries, random thrift store paperbacks, and unfinished poems.

"Ode to 180 pairs of white gloves" is after Lorraine O'Grady.

"I dreamt you at the Tate" appears in *The Rumpus* (April 2019).

"Declination" appears in *New Delta Review* as "Notice" (Spring 2019). It is after Bernadette Mayer, written as part of a *Midwinter Day* writing group organized by Becca Klaver.

"If gold, your figure as mirror on the ground is" appears in *Poetry* (October 2018).

Nine poems, including "The world says not to expect the world," appear in *The American Poetry Review* (July/August 2018).

"Ode to the accuracy of intuition" is after Martha Rosler.

"Common miracles" is after Bebel Gilberto and Wendell Berry.

"Double life" is for Erika.

"I slept when I couldn't move" appears in *Tin House* (Summer 2019) and is after Alice Notley's *In the Pines*. It also meditates on so-called conversion disorders that can occur during fibromyalgia flare-ups.

My deepest appreciation to my steadfast friends, family, University of Denver cohort, colleagues, and literary community: you know who you are, and I could not do this without you. Endless thanks to my sister Kim, for asking to hear new poems, for listening to this work all the way through—I love you. Thanks also to my teachers, editors, and writing compatriots, Dr. Tayana Hardin, Eleni Sikelianos, Matthew and Tin House, and to The Grind Writers Group—a treasure. Thank you to Ariel Robello, Monika Woods, Kima Jones, and Allison Conner. Thank you to my students, for your understanding and for the challenge.